CONTENTS

CW01426363

PREFACE

This guide is complementary to my blog, which includes more tips and information on achieving success as a freelance graphic designer, such as creating passive income and adopting the growth mindset. It's updated regularly, so please be sure to check it out, thank you!

— *John Poh, fraphic.com*

STEP 0: BEFORE WE BEGIN

Hey there! First off, I just want to thank you for purchasing this guide — your support means a lot to me.

Let's get the introductions out of the way. I'm John, a freelance graphic designer based in Singapore who has been working exclusively online for the past 6 years. I remember before I took the plunge into freelancing, I was jobless and living with my parents. Even though I graduated from college with a degree in social sciences, it was basically a paper qualification with few career prospects where I lived.

I was lost in life and finding it hard to make ends meet. The bills were piling up and I couldn't keep relying on my parents for financial assistance. I knew I had to get a job sooner rather than later, but grinding my life away at a 9 to 5 office job just didn't appeal to me.

And then a thought came to me — what if there was a way for me to make money while doing what I love?

I always have a passion for graphic design. Designs that make beautiful use of type, color, form and image have always inspired me throughout my life. I have also heard heard stories of graphic designers who were able to turn their passion into successful careers through freelancing.

I thought that if they could do it, maybe it's not impossible for me. After all, as a twenty-something what do I have to lose? As such, I made the decision to actively pursue my passion and begin my journey as a freelance graphic designer.

I haven't looked back since.

The last few years have blessed me with many valuable lessons — both good and bad — which guided me on the path to success. Along the way I have worked with people from all walks of life on hundreds of different projects. Some were great to work with. Others less so. But they all taught me the importance of building and nurturing long-lasting relationships.

For me, success means having a relatively stable income and living comfortably off it. I have had dry spells when work was harder to come by, but now that I have established a client base, I'm able to make around 4,000 USD a month quite consistently. In fact, you might be even more surprised to learn that I actually started my journey without any knowledge in graphic design, or even much of a budget.

If someone like me who started with nothing could do it, then you can also achieve the same — or even higher — level of success.

By picking up this guide, you have expressed your intention and motivation to make money online as a freelance graphic designer. Kudos to you! In addition, you have one big advantage over me — which is that I'm here to guide you every step of the way and prevent you from making the same mistakes I did.

My focus in creating this guide is to teach you how to build your portfolio and market your services so you can land your first client as easily and quickly as possible.

Everything you will read here is based on my own experiences as primarily a logo designer. While I have worked on many other types of graphic design jobs, I noticed that there is always a big demand for logo design, especially with all the startups popping up nowadays. And with all businesses and brands, the first thing they usually need is a well-designed logo. As such, you will have more opportunities and have an easier time getting clients if you start out as a logo designer.

At the same time, that doesn't mean you shouldn't grab any other opportunities that come your way. Who knows, one of them might be your golden ticket to success.

By following these steps, you are almost guaranteed to achieve success as a freelance graphic designer. I said 'almost', because there are a couple of factors that go beyond the scope of this guide. The first — and perhaps the most important — is how strong your portfolio is, which in turn depends on how proficient you are in your graphic design skills. If you don't know anything about graphic design, then I highly urge you to master the fundamentals of graphic design first before you build on your portfolio.

Don't know where and how to begin learning graphic design? Not to worry, later in this guide I will introduce some of the free methods I used when I was starting out.

Achieving success as a freelance graphic designer also depends on how well you can manage relationships with your clients. You will certainly face situations when a project goes south or a client treats you poorly. While it's easy to get emotional, remember that staying professional is key to succeeding in the long run. Always strive to deliver the best possible work to all your clients, regardlesss of how they treat you. Consequently, satisfied clients will not only come back to you with more work, they will most likely refer your services to their friends and family as well.

Otherwise, it's about staying motivated and having the fortitude to overcome any challenges that stand in your way. Are you ready to make money online as a freelance graphic designer? Let's get started!

Quick Update

I wrote this guide in 2017, so some of the information has become outdated. As such, I have revised and updated the content in this second edition. Spelling and grammatical errors should also be fixed for a better reading experience.

STEP 1: MAKING THE NECESSARY PREPARATIONS

Step 1.1

Learning The Fundamentals Of Graphic Design

Here I'm assuming that you don't have any prior education in graphic design, otherwise feel free to skip this part.

I think it goes without saying that having a strong foundation in graphic design is vital to your success as a freelance graphic designer. You might think that not having went to school for graphic design would negatively affect your chances of getting hired for projects.

I'm here to tell you that's not the case and that it's not your education, but your portfolio that's the most important. And in order to build a strong portfolio, you first have to take time to learn and master the fundamentals of graphic design.

I will suggest a couple of ways you can pick up those fundamentals for free, but thereafter you will have to do your own legwork.

1.1.a. YOUTUBE

If you are looking to learn graphic design for free then YouTube is your best friend, with videos for nearly everything you need to know on the subject. Also, watching videos is probably a more interesting way to learn than reading through a textbook for most of us.

My personal recommendations include *The Futur*, *Satori Graphics*, and *Will Patterson*, but feel free to seek out and subscribe other channels that you feel will be useful in your learning journey.

1.1.b. LIBRARY

If you are fortunate enough like me to have a local library in your area, then you should easily have access to books on graphic design that you can borrow and learn from.

I remember spending hours a day at my local library, reading through books on graphic design and taking notes as I go. While YouTube is great and all, I find that I learn better through the written word. In any case, it's always better to learn from multiple sources to widen your knowledge.

1.1.c. ONLINE

A quick Google search on 'graphic design for beginners' yielded tons of results, many of which should be useful in helping you pick up the fundamentals of graphic design.

The good thing about online resources is that you can learn anytime and anywhere as long as you have access to the internet, so you can choose to learn whenever is most comfortable for you.

Step 1.2

Choosing A Name For Your Brand

Now that you have a good understanding on the fundamentals of graphic design, it's time to start think about how you want to brand yourself as a freelancer. First, you will need to choose a name to identify your brand. Having a good name will help to get you noticed as a freelance graphic designer. Essentially it comes down to using your own name or a business name.

Making a decision can be hard, but it depends on what your long-term goals are and the message you are looking to convey.

Using your own name gives a more personal touch to your brand. However, it might not work as well if you are ever planning to expand into a business. Having a business name can make you look more legitimate, but it makes your clients feel like they are dealing with an agency — along with higher costs.

In addition, there's also the consideration of how clear and recognizable the name you choose is. This applies more to personal names, since it might be hard to leave a lasting impression if you have a name that's not easy to remember.

Furthermore, even after you think you have finally come up with a good name, oftentimes a Google search will reveal that it has already been taken, along with the associated domain name. While you can still go with the name you decided on, it usually means having to compete with an already established brand, which might not be worth your time and effort. Back to square one then.

In my case I wanted to incorporate 'John' into my brand name, and luckily for me 'Johnery' was available as a .com domain, so it was a no-brainer.

Obviously the name you choose will be different, but you should try to make it as short and unique as possible. For illustration purposes, we will be using MY BRAND as our brand name moving forward.

Step 1.3

Saving Up Some Money

Let's get something out of the way first. Although it's definitely possible to start your freelancing journey with no budget as per the title of this guide, investing in professional web services and a graphics tablet will yield you many dividends in the long term.

In my case, I'm spending around 20 USD to register my domain on NameCheap and close to 100 USD to host my portfolio site on SiteGround. These are annual fees, so monthly I'm paying around 10 USD — which is about the cost of a McDonald's meal here in Singapore, and something I can easily skip.

Also, I recommend setting up your portfolio site on Squarespace if you don't know anything about web design and development,. We will talk more about this later on.

As for a graphics tablet, I went with a brand new Wacom Intuos Draw that cost around 50 USD. Based on my experience you will usually start a project by sketching out ideas and coming up with concepts. The traditional pencil and paper is the most straightforward and cheapest option. However, with communication being mostly done online you will need to digitally present your sketches to the client. Of course, there are solutions such as using a scanner or camera, but it can get tedious after a while, especially if the client requests for multiple rounds of revisions.

A graphics tablet allows you to draw digitally using a stylus, though you do need some practice to get used to drawing on a computer screen. Wacom is the most popular brand for graphic tablets right now. While there are other brands on the market, you might run into driver and pen problems as reported by some users.

For a cheaper option, consider getting a refurbished or second-hand tablet. Remember, you are only looking to sketch out concepts as part of your design process, not come up with fancy illustrations, so there's no need to get something too high-end.

As an estimate I would recommend you have around 200 USD in hand before moving forward with this guide. I'm not going to spoonfeed you on how you can make that amount here, but as an example consider doing odd jobs such as mowing the lawn or selling your unwanted items.

You might feel that 200 USD is a lot, but having the abovementioned items will make it easier for you to achieve success as a freelance graphic designer.

Step 1.4

Downloading A Few Open Source Software

Although Adobe is the industry standard among graphic designers, do you know that there are some open source alternatives that are completely free to download and use? I started out with them and am actually still using them for the majority of my work even though I have an Adobe subscription. Let's take a look at the three open source software that I'm currently using and you will likely need as a freelance graphic designer.

If you are curious, an open source software contains code that can be accessed and modified by anyone. Such projects promote collaboration and sharing. As such, they are usually free to use, with software-specific add-ons available to personalize your user experience.

1.4.a. GIMP

For a decent Photoshop alternative, check out the GNU Image Manipulation Program (or GIMP for short). It's almost 2 decades old, with new and improved features being added with each build.

I don't use GIMP much in my workflow since I don't do a lot of image manipulation, but it's a useful software to have, especially when you have to blend different images together with layer modes. GIMP's official website has tutorials that introduce you to the interface and walk you through some basic image manipulation techniques.

1.4.b. Inkscape

If you want to focus on designing logos then Inkscape is pretty much your bread and butter when it comes to creating vector graphics, which are basically images that can be scaled to different resolutions without losing quality.

Based on my experience most clients will request for their logos to be designed in vector, as they can then repurpose the vector source files for various branding purposes.

Don't forget to visit Inkscape's official website to find out more about the software. Since you will be using Inkscape a lot, I recommend that you go through all the tutorials there, which covers all the basic features and everything you need to know to get started.

1.4.c. MyPaint

Assuming that you did purchase a graphics tablet, you will need a drawing software to produce and display the sketches on screen. For that I recommend MyPaint. The software is easy to use and has a simple interface, so you will be get the hang of it in no time.

MyPaint's main draw (no pun intended) is definitely its unlimited canvas, allowing you to sketch as much as you want on a single page — very useful for brainstorming and conceptualization.

Step 1.5

Creating A Couple Of Accounts

1.5.a. PayPal

As a freelance graphic designer you will need a fast and safe way to receive money from clients. As such, having a PayPal account is pretty much a must simply because clients can then pay you securely from anywhere in the world and in just seconds — all they need is your email address. In addition, clients can pay by credit card if they don't have an account on PayPal.

Since I'm located outside the United States, which is where most of my clients are from, I need a payment service that not only facilities the transfer of money, but also allows me to withdraw funds to my local bank without any issues.

Even if you are based in the United States, some of your clients might be from overseas, where PayPal is pretty much the only international service available to them.

Furthermore, having all your transactions in one account makes it much easier for you to do your books and pay your taxes (depending on the laws in your country).

PayPal does charge a fee for each transaction, which means you will have to forgo a small percentage of your income. Nobody likes to part with their hard-earned money, but I feel it's a small price to pay for the security and ease of access that PayPal provides. In fact, I have clients who pay me a bit extra to cover the fees even without my asking, so my advice would be not to worry about this too much.

Also, PayPal has been taking steps to protect freelancers over the years. If you need an example, one of my clients previously filed a chargeback (amounting to 250 USD) through their credit card company against me, claiming that I didn't deliver on what they asked for — when I clearly did.

Fortunately, I kept all records of the project and the conversations that transpired between us, and PayPal was able to work with me to refute the chargeback based on the evidence provided. So if you do face a chargeback in the future, be assured that PayPal will do everything within their means to help you get your money back.

One question you may have is whether to set up personal or business PayPal account. For a freelancer, a personal account is more than sufficient, and it's what I have been using. You can set up a business account and have access to additional benefits on PayPal, but you will have to register as a business with the relevant authorities (depending on where you are from), which usually involves quite a bit of paperwork. In short, it's a tedious process, when the time could be better spent on building your portfolio or reaching out to clients instead.

1.5.b. Gmail

Communication is key to the design process. If done well, it improves client relationships and ensures that projects go without a hitch.

I might be an expection among freelancers, but email is my main form of communication. One reason is that I'm located in a totally different timezone from my clients who are mostly based in the United States, so practically it can be hard to schedule a video call between both parties.

In addition, video calls aren't really cost and time effective for me. Conversely I can check my emails anytime and anywhere — it encourages clients to get straight to the point with the information they provide, thus streamlining the design process.

Gmail is the obvious choice when it comes to email. You can't go wrong with 15 GB of storage, less spam, and mobile access. I would advise that you create an account strictly for your freelancing needs, with an email that incorporates your brand name such as *contact.MYBRAND@gmail.com*.

1.5.c.1. Dropbox

One day, I was working hard on a project — only to have my laptop die on me, causing me to lose all my files. Unfortunately such incidents can and do happen from time to time. In order to protect your files, having a backup system is very important for a freelance graphic designer.

Here's where Dropbox comes in. It's free up to 2 GB of storage space and allows you to retain revisions of your files as you work on them, while syncing those files and revisions between different machines and for multiple users.

You might think 2 GB is not a lot, but I only used up all that space after 2 years of freelancing. After that, you can either upgrade to Dropbox Plus (1TB at 8.25 USD a month), or simply sign up for a new account with a different email address.

1.5.c.2. Google Drive

Similarly, since you probably have already created a Google account while signing up for Gmail, why not make use of Google Drive as well? Unlike Dropbox, Google Drive offers up to 15 GB of storage for free, though that storage is shared among the other Google services such as Google Photos and Gmail.

I'm someone who believes in backing up my backups, so I always make sure to regularly back up my files on both Dropbox and Google Drive. As the saying goes, better safe than sorry.

1.5.d. Reddit

Reddit might seem like an unlikely choice for finding work, but as a highly popular social networking service it's actually where I'm getting most of my clients from. Furthermore, with subreddits such as r/graphic_design, Reddit makes it easy for you to share ideas and pick the brains of other graphic designers.

It literally takes less than a minute to sign up for a Reddit account. For your username, I suggest choosing something professional that is based on your brand and what you do, such as MYBRANDCreatives — something like IamASuperDesigner112 probably won't attract any clients.

Once done, your next step is to subscribe to the following subreddits: *r/logorequests*, *r/forhire*, *r/designjobs*, and *r/freelance_forhire*.

That's it for now. We will be making use of these subreddits later on in this guide.

STEP 2: BUILDING A PORTFOLIO OF WORK

As a freelance graphic designer your portfolio is key to getting hired — which means you need a good amount of projects to showcase your skills and experience to clients. However, self-initiated work is often substandard and doesn't translate well into real world situations.

On the other hand, you won't have a portfolio to show clients if you don't work with them to come up with designs in the first place — it's certainly a chicken and egg situation. One approach is to work for free until you have built a portfolio of work, which has the advantage of allowing you to gain some useful firsthand working experience in the process.

At the same time, it's not a good idea to associate your brand with free services. Since you will only doing this temporarily, picking a simple and generic name should suffice. Consider creating separate Gmail and Reddit accounts (repeat steps 1.5.b. and 1.5.d.) to interact with these clients.

I do touch on a few other ways to build a portfolio of work on my blog, but the ones I'll be sharing next are based on what worked for me. Also, we will be focusing on creating a portfolio as a logo designer from here on, so keep that in mind.

Step 2.1
REDDIT

I started out by providing free services on a subreddit called *r/freedesign* which, as its name implies, is created for clients seeking free graphic design services and designers looking to work pro bono to expand their portfolios. In fact, one of the clients liked my work so much he paid me 150 USD after the job was done. It was my first paycheck, and really taught me the value of quality work.

Unfortunately, that subreddit has closed down a couple of years ago, so we will have to move on to the next method to build your portfolio, namely design contests such as 99designs.

Step 2.2
99DESIGNS

99designs is probably the world's largest marketplace for graphic design. Clients hold contests in different design categories, with designers submitting their best entries. A cash payment is then awarded to the winning designer.

You will find many different clients and thousands of contests on 99designs. A design brief is required for every contest so you can better tailor your submission to client specifications.

As a logo designer, 99designs connects you to clients from all walks of life. As such, you will find logo requests that differ greatly in scope. Taking them on gives you the chance to push your creativity and create work that is rich in variety.

A diverse portfolio highlights your adaptability — something clients often look for when hiring a logo designer. Being experienced in creating different types and styles of logos will help you appeal to a wider audience as well.

While money isn't a priority for now, by focusing on creating quality logos you might actually have a good chance of winning some contests. In addition, joining a contest gives you the chance to check out submissions from other designers — it's definitely interesting to see how they can process the same information and produce vastly different results.

STEP 3: SELECTING AND SHOWCASING YOUR BEST PORTFOLIO PIECES

As mentioned earlier, I mostly went with *r/freedesign* to build my portfolio of work since I had an easier time getting in touch with clients than 99designs. In the end, I had about 50 portfolio pieces before starting my selection process.

Similarly, you should now have a few projects under your belt, which brings us to the next question of which ones you should include in your portfolio.

As mentioned previously, let's focus on logo design for your portfolio. I suggest choosing quality pieces that are diverse in scope — you want to show that you can easily adapt your skills to meet the client's needs. Casting your net as wide as possible gives you a better chance of netting (no pun intended) your first client as soon as possible.

Usually a lot of work is involved during the design process that clients don't get to see, such as how you came up with the concepts, why you chose this particular color scheme, and so on. As such, it's not a bad idea to offer some insight for each portfolio piece, which can include notes and annotations, case studies if you want to provide more details, or better yet, testimonials from the clients themselves.

Consider taking advantage of mockups, which are visual representations of how a design will look and function in real life using artistic renders. Mockups allow you to showcase your projects in context, making them more visually engaging to the clients. You will find many resources available on sites such as GraphicBurger and Pixeden. However, note that most of the mockup templates require you to have Adobe Photoshop.

STEP 4: HOSTING YOUR PORTFOLIO SITE ON SQUARESPACE

Just a heads up, this section isn't actually based on my own experience, but rather what I feel would work best for you. In my case, because I know some HTML and CSS, I decided to use a Bootstrap template and customize it to my needs. This approach gave me a lot more control over how my portfolio site works and looks.

On the other hand, coding is oftentimes a tedious and frustrating process, and the purpose of this guide is to help you make money as a freelance graphic designer as easily and quickly as possible. As such, I recommend Squarespace instead, which offers a user-friendly and versatile experience so you can host and create a beautiful and fully functional portfolio site — even without any prior knowledge in web design and development.

With Squarespace you don't have to worry about touching a line of code with their drag-and-drop fuctionality, which means you can focus your efforts on freelancing and getting clients as soon as possible.

Currently Squarespace gives you 7 designer templates to choose from that are catered for creative services. All templates are responsive, meaning your portfolio site will look good no matter what devices your clients use. In addition, Squarespace's seamless social integrations make it easy for you to reach out to a wider audience.

These templates are just a starting point though — with hundreds of customizable features you can style your portfolio site to look any way you want later on.

Personally I'm quite a fan of the York template, its stacked landing page summarizes your work, while the case-study page tells the story behind each project.

If you still can't decide whether to go with Squarespace, they offer a 14-day free trial as soon as you sign up so you have a chance to try out their features. However, in order for your portfolio to go live you would need to purchase a personal account at 16 USD per month (billed annually or 23 USD month to month). It comes with unlimited bandwidth and a drag-and-drop editor among other features — more than enough for your portfolio site.

Furthermore, all Squarespace sites on an annual billing plan include one free custom domain, which is a nice bonus. Your domain is free for the first year starting from the date it's registered.

After starting your free trial, I suggest going through Squarespace's video tutorial series, which will teach you how to get your web presence up and running. And if you need inspiration on how to design your portfolio site, be sure to check out the examples that are showcased there.

If you have done your own research, you might have heard about using WordPress to set up your portfolio site, meaning that you will have to purchase a hosting plan (which costs around 5 to 10 USD a month) from a provider such as SiteGround. Granted it's cheaper than hosting on Squarespace, but assuming that you aren't knowledgeable in content management systems you will likely be overwhelmed by all the technical work that goes into installing software, choosing the right plugins and themes, and implementing basic web development.

You don't have to worry about all that with Squarespace. Basically you just have to sign up for an account, choose a template, and Squarespace will guide you through the process from start to finish. Also, WordPress is primarily designed as a blogging platform, whereas

Squarespace is created with creative professionals like you in mind.

In the end, I definitely recommend hosting your portfolio site on Squarespace. However, if you would like to explore other options, I have written more about them on my blog.

Step 4.1

Making Your Portfolio Site Work For You

Although Squarespace takes care of most of the design aspects for you, you still have to understand some basic principles of web design in order to make the most out of your portfolio site.

Let's take a step back from design and talk about marketing. Call to action, as its name suggests, is an image or line of text that prompts users to take action and convert them into paying customers. In this case, your call to action (usually a 'contact me' button) should get clients to contact you with more information.

In order to increase sales and get more clients, you have to design your portfolio site well. For that it's a good idea to establish visual hierarchy in a page, starting with elements that draw the most attention. For instance, how a word in **bold** catches your eye.

Color influences the first impression. For example, navy appears serious, but not drab. Yellow is warm and uplifts the spirits. Black emits a strong message. At the same time, colors should support and not overpower your content, so it's a good idea to simplify your color choices. Stick to basic color schemes and use them effectively to showcase your projects and guide clients to your call to action. Using color accents is a good way to draw users to specific content that you want to highlight as well.

Your eyes will get tired if you are reading something that's all cramped together on a page. Such content will be much more readable if different elements are separated by spacing. In web design, such spacing is referred to as whitespace. Knowing how and when to use whitespace will allow you to deliver an enjoyable experience to clients by improving readability and giving elements on a page room to breathe. The result is a website that is elegant and balanced.

A picture may say a thousand words. However, most websites rely on text to bring the message across. Type and typography are often overlooked, but when done well will bring the design of your portfolio site to the next level.

In choosing typefaces, Sans Serif fonts such as Arial and Verdana are easier to read online. Try not to overdo it with the typefaces — keep it to below three so the design of your portfolio site is more streamlined.

For typography, consider using font sizes and weights to create a clear structure. As with whitespace, keep your letters and words properly spaced so they are easy to read.

Unity is about forming strong relationships between elements and pages, thus creating a brand identity that's consistent throughout the site. It can be as simple as using the same colors and typefaces throughout your portfolio site, or placing related elements closer together.

By applying these principles, your portfolio site will look much more professional to clients, which greatly improves their impression of you as a freelance graphic designer.

STEP 5: PLANNING FOR SUCCESS

Now that your portfolio site is up and running, it's tempting to start looking for your first client. However, diving right in without a plan can be a recipe for disaster. Instead, I want you to come up with a plan for success, which should include the following:

Step 5.1

Reaffirming Your Goals And Objectives

It's important to set goals and objectives so you can give yourself a sense of purpose and direction. Goals and objectives are often used interchangeably, but they usually mean different things. Goals represent your aspirations as a freelance graphic designer and the direction you want to take, while objectives are the steps you will take to reach those goals, and are typically measurable and quantifiable.

Having goals encourages you to think of your ideal future as a freelance graphic designer and motivates you to turn that vision into reality, while the objectives you set should guide you towards achieving those goals and to success. Start with the big picture and get more specific as you go further into the planning process.

At the same time, circumstances can and will change. As such, you should reevaluate and update your plan from time to time, so as to make sure that you are still heading in the right direction.

I suggest making some short-term goals for now so you can gain momentum on your path to success. In my case, my first goal was to make 300 USD in my first 3 months, which I was able to meet after much hard work. I increased that amount gradually thereafter until I got to where I am now.

Step 5.2

Finding Your Target Audience

Clients come in all shapes and sizes, from individuals to CEOs of notable corporations. The question is, just how wide of a net should you cast?

Like I mentioned earlier, it's wise to cater to a wider demographic when you are just starting out. Understand that high-profile clients are probably out of your reach, since they usually work with high-end design studios with years of experience. Conversely, do your best to avoid low-balling clients trying to hire for cheap — consider a target audience that is somewhere in between. On one end, you have a small business owner willing to invest in rebranding. On the other, an individual ready to pay well to develop his or her personal brand. It's a good idea to have a range of clients so you can better develop your design and customer service skills, while adding diversity to your portfolio.

Step 5.3

What Services Are You Providing?

Once you have identified your target audience, it's time to start thinking about the types of services you will be offering. As the saying goes, never put all your eggs in one basket. There will be times when your services are less in demand, and such 'dry spells' might result in financial trouble.

Diversification is definitely beneficial to a freelance graphic designer. Specializing in at least 2 services allows you to expand your client base and reduce the risks of freelancing — if a service isn't doing well you will have alternatives to rely on for income.

As mentioned earlier, one of your services should be logo design since it's usually always in demand. The other depends on what you are passionate in, but I suggest you focus your efforts on being a logo designer first and building a client base from there. In the end, sustainability is the name of the game — the services you choose to offer should ensure your success in the long run.

Step 5.4

Pricing Your Services

As a freelance graphic designer you decide how much to price your services. The question is, how much is enough? You can't magically grab numbers from thin air. Instead, consider sharing your work on places such as Behance and Dribbble, where you can get critiques and see how well your work fares against others. If you are getting mostly positive feedback, then you can probably afford to charge more for your services since your work is of better quality than the competition.

If not, think about setting lower prices for now while you improve your skills and knowledge. Don't be afraid to reach out to veterans and get advice on how much you should charge.

In any case, once you have a number in mind the next step would be to map out your pricing strategy. 120 USD is a good starting point from my own experience quoting hundreds of clients over the years. Remember, never negotiate on rate — only in scope. We will talk more about creating a package based on the client's budget later on.

Step 5.5

Deciding Whether To Use A Contract

If you have been to my blog, you would understand that it's never a bad idea to have a contract. Having a valid agreement not only protects you and the client in case of contingencies, but also keeps the project on track. Furthermore, stating the terms and conditions deters those who are looking to exploit your services, thus reducing issues of nonpayment.

On the flipside, contracts can't protect anything unless enforced. You need money, patience and most importantly, evidence to disprove payment claims. It's almost always not worth it, especially when dealing with international clients.

As of right now, I haven't been using contracts for the past year — and pretty much nothing has changed. I haven't been shortchanged 99% of the time, and even if the project has expanded in scope, the client was usually understanding enough to increase their budget.

STEP 6: GETTING YOUR FIRST CLIENT

In this guide we will only be using Reddit to get clients since it's what worked for me and probably will work for you. It's one of the biggest and busiest websites. In 2022 it had 1.8 billion visitors — a vast market for a freelance graphic designer.

If you have been following the steps so far, you should be familiar with how subreddits work on Reddit. We will be looking at subreddits where you can sell and promote your services, as well as strategies to maximize your presence on these subreddits.

Before we begin, be warned that spam posts are a big no-no. No one likes spam, and spamming your services repeatedly is guaranteed to get you banned from a subreddit. Most of the subreddits have rules that disallow you from posting more than once a week.

I have had the experience of having one of my posts removed by a moderator of a subreddit because I last posted six days ago instead of the mandatory seven. If you have any questions, don't hesitate to message the moderators.

Since it's so easy to create a Reddit account, you are likely to run into scammers who will exploit your services. As such, you should proactively take steps to protect yourself as a freelancer.

First, check the potential client's post history. Be wary of someone who has a brand new account, or has been posting vulgar comments. Next, try to avoid spec work, which is when designers are asked to submit their designs as entries, and only the 'winning' entry is given payment. Such practice is frowned upon by designers, since it usually means you won't get paid in the end — clients should always hire designers based on the quality of their portfolios.

Your first step to promoting on Reddit is to have a well-written text post advertising your services. Take some time to review both your headline and description. The headline is what draws clients in and decides whether they will be interested enough to read your post. It should not only be simple and to the point, but also have a 'hook' — something to draw the client's attention. For example, instead of 'Logo Designer Looking for Work', try 'High Quality Logos by an Experienced Designer'.

For the description, be sure to include as many details as possible. Don't forget to describe your design process and workflow. In order to minimize disagreements later on, you want clients to know you better and understand how you work. It's also a good idea to have a few testimonials from redditors whom you have worked with previously to establish credibility. And of course, don't forget to provide your contact information and a link to your portfolio.

Finally, format your post so it's neatly organized and easy to read. If you need more help, you can always check out the posts from other graphic designers. As an example, here's a well-written copy by SanRedStudios:

Hey there!

A little bio about the designer called me.

My name is San Red and I'm a 23 year old guy from Sweden. I am the co-founder of a web agency but on the side I freelance doing mostly logo work (check out my portfolio here). I also study on the side for a Masters in Science and Engineering (majoring in computer science) at the Royal Institute of Technology.

I also have a pet bird because someone told me designers have to be eccentric.

MY PROCESS

I work completely after my clients' needs. I will do my research on your company/brand and adapt after it. You can be as involved as you like, if you have a specific idea in mind, great! I will do everything I can to make it a reality. And if you should not have any ideas and would like to grant me free hands, that's ok too! I love being creative.

REVISIONS

I know most designers have a set amount of revisions but I don't do that. I will keep working until you are satisfied.

PRICE

The price isn't set in stone. I mostly freelance to keep my creative juices flowing so it won't be terribly expensive. I can tell you that it will not go above $250, and rarely has it ever gone above $200.

EXPERIENCE ON REDDIT

I have had quite a few clients from Reddit and it has all gone smoothly!

Here is a testimonial by a previous client […]

DELIVERY

All my logos are of course created in vector format. When the designing process is done and it's time to deliver, I'll send it to you in any file type you'd like. I'll also help you out with cropping, resizing or whatever else you'd like help with afterwards. The standard files I send to my clients are these: .eps .ai .png. svg. And if you should want some other type, simply ask!

OTHER

I also do a lot of other work, pretty much any web dev and graphic design work. Including business cards, letterheads, merchandise, packaging, smartphone applications, UI/UX design consultation, website development and anything else you can think of. If you need anything, just ask!

Feel free to inquire about anything you might be wondering about. Just send me a PM or you can find my email on my website. I don't bite!

And again, you can find my portfolio here.

Unfortunately it's easy for your post to get drowned out within hours since information moves so fast on Reddit. Remember, you usually only get one chance a week to post on a subreddit, so choosing the right time to post is very important. Do your research and find out when a subreddit is most active.

Subreddits that cater to businesses, such as *r/forhire*, usually have the most active users in the mornings and afternoons — typical office hours. Also, almost half of redditors are from the United States, so you should take time zones into consideration, especially if like me you are located on the other side of the world.

Simultaneously, clients are also posting job listings and looking to hire designers on these subreddits. Listings usually move fast, so it's a good idea to check regularly to be the first to reach out and stay ahead of the competition. As the saying goes, the early bird catches the worm.

Finally, let's take a look at the subreddits where you can promote your services. The first subreddit is *r/forhire*, a place for businesses looking to hire freelancers. It's very popular, so you are guaranteed to find job listings for graphic designers every day.

Next up, we have *r/designjobs*. As the name implies it's catered to design jobs and projects, so expect much more competition. On the other hand, your post will generate more interest since clients are specifically looking to hire graphic designers.

We also have *r/freelance_forhire*, another job bulletin for freelancers. It's relatively new and not as popular as the aforementioned two subreddits, but more promotion is never a bad thing.

While I have provided you with three subreddits that I usually use, you should also take the initiative and seek out subreddits frequented by your target audience. For example, if you are looking to work with startups then consider promoting your services on *r/startups*. Similarly, to connect with women entrepreneurs, try *r/ladybusiness*.

STEP 7: COMPLETING YOUR FIRST PROJECT

Now it's just a matter of waiting for a client to reach out to you, be it through Reddit or email. I will be using one of my previous projects as an example so you can better understand how the whole thing would usually play out. First, the client will message you expressing their interest in hiring your services. In this case, I'm John and let's call the client Jason.

Hi there!

I'm starting up a podcast and would love to have a logo for social media accounts as well as for the website I'm setting up to host it. I was wondering if you'd be interested in/available for such a thing, and if so, hoping to talk pricing with you.

Hope to hear back soon!

Thanks!

/

Hi Jason,

Thanks for your interest! I would love to work with you to design the logo for your podcast.

Feel free to provide me with the details and we'll go from there. I look forward to hearing back from you.

/

John,

Thank you for the prompt reply! I greatly appreciate it. Here's a quick rundown of what the podcast is about[...]

We're in need of a logo with a more professional feel than our competitors, but doesn't take itself too seriously. Your "Cardboard Arcade" and "Forted Workshop" logos are perfect examples of the direction I have in mind (though maybe with a little more use of color). We'll be using it for Facebook/Twitter profile pictures, as well as the website we'll be setting up to host the podcast.

How much would you charge for a service like this?

I look forward to hearing back from you!

/

Jason,

Sounds good. Do you have a budget in mind as well? If so, feel free to let me know and I'll be happy to take it into consideration before providing you with a quote.

/

John,

The budget my brother and I currently have in mind is $200.

Let us know what you have in mind and we'll try to work with you on it.

Thank you!

/

Jason,

No problem, I'm comfortable with your budget of $200. It'll include the source vector files as deliverables, 3 initial concepts, and as many revisions as necessary until the design meets your expectations.

As for payment, is PayPal alright with you? I'll collect a 20% deposit, 30% after you approve the concept, and the rest once everything is finalized.

Here you want to get the pricing out in the open sooner than later.

In negotiations, the first party to say a number is usually in a less advantageous position. My approach is to ask for the client's budget as soon as possible without stating my own rates. Remember when I asked you to have a number in mind based on the value you attach to your services? Well once you know the client's budget you can then tailor your package accordingly.

At the same time, the client might not be willing to reveal their budget or don't have one. In this case, go with a pricing that you are comfortable with and see if they are willing to work with that number.

What should you do if the client wants to go cheaper or their budget is too low for you? First, try to see if they are open to increasing their budget. If not, you have the choice to respectfully decline the project. It's best not to work with clients who are looking to hire for cheap, as they will only exploit your services in the end.

Don't fall into the trap of undercutting the value of your services to pay the bills. It never works out well, unless a project really appeals to you. You will devalue yourself as a graphic designer, and taking on such projects will only make you feel bitter and underutilized.

In fact, clients will respect you more if you can get them to see you as a professional and that they are paying for good service. Ultimately, it's about trust between both parties and charging a fair price that is in line with the value of your services.

Once the client has agreed on the price, **always** ask for a deposit — I cannot stress this enough. Usually I would go for a 40% deposit and the rest once everything is finalized. I find that this approach work best to protect the interests of both parties.

After that, the rest of the process should be quite straightforward and usually involves conceptualization and exploration, communication with the client, and execution of the final design.

Of course every client is different, so you will have to navigate your way through situations such as delays in communication or payment, negative feedback and so on, but they do get more manageable over time. My advice would be to just take things in your stride and try not to let your emotions get in the way.

WHAT'S NEXT?

Assuming you have been following all the steps above, you should be close to earning your first paycheck. Now it's just a matter of developing a routine (remember to promote yourself regularly on Reddit) and staying motivated.

If you would like more tips and advice on achieving success as a freelance graphic designer, be sure to check out my blog. Also, if you have any further questions after reading this guide, feel free to leave a comment on my blog and I'll be more than happy to help as best as I can.

I hope you enjoy this guide, and commend you for taking the courage to walk a different path in life!

Printed in Great Britain
by Amazon

38077193R00025